Wild Science Careers

STORM SCIENTIST

Careers Chasing Severe Weather

TIMOTHY R. GAFFNEY

E **Enslow Publishers, Inc.**
40 Industrial Road
Box 398
Berkeley Heights, NJ 07922
USA

http://www.enslow.com

Library of Congress Cataloging-in-Publication Data

Gaffney, Timothy R.

    Storm scientist : careers chasing severe weather / by Timothy R. Gaffney.

        p. cm. — (Wild science careers)

    Summary: "Explores careers in weather science using several examples of real-life scientists"—Provided by publisher.

    Includes bibliographical references and index.

    ISBN-13: 978-0-7660-3050-3

    1. Meteorology—Vocational guidance—Juvenile literature. 2. Meteorologists—Juvenile literature. 3. Weather—Juvenile literature. I. Title.

    QC869.5.G34 2009

    551.5023—dc22

                        2008004681

ISBN-10: 0-7660-3050-4

Printed in the United States of America

10 9 8 7 6 5 4 3 2 1

To Our Readers: We have done our best to make sure all Internet Addresses in this book were active and appropriate when we went to press. However, the author and the publisher have no control over and assume no liability for the material available on those Internet sites or on other Web sites they may link to. Any comments or suggestions can be sent by e-mail to comments@enslow.com or to the address on the back cover.

♻ Enslow Publishers, Inc., is committed to printing our books on recycled paper. The paper in every book contains 10% to 30% post-consumer waste (PCW). The cover board on the outside of each book contains 100% PCW. Our goal is to do our part to help young people and the environment too!

Photo Credits: 2008 © University Corporation for Atmospheric Research, p. 50; Associated Press, pp. 1, 6, 35; Center for Severe Weather Research, p. 16; Courtesy, Dr. Gary Hufford, p. 36; Danny Cheresnick, Center for Severe Weather Research, p. 4; Enslow Publishers, p. 14; Eric Nguyen/Photo Researchers, Inc., p. 10; Eurelios/Photo Researchers, Inc., p. 8; George Janson, Colorado State University, pp. 24, 26; Herb Stein, Center for Severe Weather Research, p. 11; Jim Reed Photography/Photo Researchers, Inc., pp. 17, 48; Jonathan Moreno, p. 67; Louise Murray/Photo Researchers, Inc., p. 91; Mark Newman/Photo Researchers, Inc., p. 45; National Oceanic and Atmospheric Administration/Department of Commerce, pp. 53, 56; Photo by Luc Rainville (APL/UW), pp. 77, 78, 83, 85, 87; Photo courtesy of Brian Russell, pp. 64, 69, 71; Randy Borys, founder of Storm Peak Lab, pp. 23, 33; Shutterstock, pp. 37, 52, 63.

Cover Photo: Associated Press

Contents

CHAPTER 1

The Quest for Knowledge

A violent storm was sweeping across western Oklahoma on May 29, 2004. Behind a screen of rain and wind-driven dust, the storm was brewing a **tornado**. No human eye could see the twister, but Dr. Joshua Wurman had an electronic eye that could peer into the heart of the storm. His eye was a special radar unit, mounted on the back of a big truck.

Wurman is a scientist who hunts tornadoes. His mobile radar unit is a special tool he made to help him hunt them. The radar unit emits radio signals and measures the echoes that bounce back. It can measure wind speeds and directions inside a storm, including the mysterious, whirling funnel of a twister. It even lets him study what is happening inside a tornado, the way a doctor might use x-rays to peer inside a patient's body.

This storm was a brute. "It was a storm [that] was very windy and kicking up a lot of dust," Wurman recalls. "We couldn't see. We had several vehicles in our fleet, and we told everybody to stay away, and we went into the storm . . . with the radar."

By 2004, Wurman had seen and studied tornadoes and violent storms more closely than most scientists. But violent storms could still spring surprises. This one was about to.

"We parked [the truck] in front of the tornado, about two to three miles away, and started scanning it [with the radar unit]. That's the usual thing we do. We'd get in front of it and let it come towards us, and at a certain time when it got too close, we would run away. . . . The tornado got less than a mile from us, so we said, 'All right, time to move.'"

Tornadoes and high winds caused this devastation in western Oklahoma.

Wurman was sealed inside a tiny cabin between the radar and the driver's cab. He was concentrating on the radar data that flowed across a computer screen. But he could tell something was wrong outside.

"We're driving south, and it's clear we're not moving on the highway. I'm yelling at my driver in front, saying, 'We can't stop here. We've got to keep moving. There's a tornado coming at us.' And he's yelling back at me, telling me he had the [gas pedal] floored, and we weren't going anywhere."

The tornado came right at them. Thanks to the radar, Wurman could see it: a tight funnel of wind whirling at 130 miles an hour. But the radar was detecting an additional threat that only later study would make clear: The truck couldn't move because the storm surrounding the tornado was packing winds of up to 180 miles an hour.

"The door got ripped off our truck. Stuff got ripped off the roof. It was getting bad quickly, and we couldn't figure it out, and we couldn't get out of it because we couldn't move the truck."[1]

Scientists who study weather use all the high-tech tools and gadgets that modern technology offers. Space satellites observe weather from above the atmosphere. Instruments at remote stations around

A weather balloon, like the one seen here in the Antarctic, can be a useful gadget for meteorologists because it can carry weather instruments.

the world tirelessly report weather conditions. Supercomputers crunch massive amounts of data to predict the behavior of weather and changes in Earth's **climate**.

But sometimes the only way to understand weather is to get right into the middle of it. And that is precisely what some scientists do. Instead of a laboratory full of gadgets, you might find them in a truck chasing tornadoes, in an airplane flying through **hurricanes**, or in a primitive hut on the remote Arctic ice.

Getting the knowledge these scientists seek can be a physical adventure. It can also be hard, dangerous work that is anything but glamorous. In the chapters that follow, the stories you will read are not just entertaining tales. The dangers they describe are real. A flight through a hurricane is not a theme park ride, after all. And a charging bear is a serious threat.

Their urge to learn, though, helps us all. The more scientists learn about weather, the better **meteorologists** can predict dangerous weather and warn us about it. The more they learn about Earth's changing climate, the better we can understand how climate change will affect us—and how we are affecting it.

CHAPTER 2

The Fury of a Twister

Why do scientists study storms? Wurman says two things mainly motivate scientists. "One is [that] we want to understand the unknown. It's that drive to explore [that] humans just have. . . . The drive to explore and learn things. The second thing is [that] we want to do good, basically. It sounds corny, but we're trying to study things that will have some value.

We study storms so we can forecast them better and warn people better."[1]

Tornado forecasting is not new. The National Weather Service credits two Air Force weather officers with making the first tornado forecast on March 25, 1948. Five days after a tornado ravaged Tinker Air Force Base in Oklahoma, Captain Robert C. Miller and Major Ernest J. Fawbush correctly predicted weather conditions were ripe for more twisters. As storms developed and swept toward the base, they issued a tornado forecast. Loose equipment was

Dr. Joshua Wurman uses his Doppler on Wheels (DOW), a truck with a special radar unit, to study tornadoes.

secured, air traffic was warned away, and people took shelter. Sure enough, a tornado roared across the base, leaving 6 million dollars in damage. But no lives were lost.[2]

Much to Learn About Twisters

Scientists have been trying to improve tornado forecasting ever since. But after half a century of research with ever-better technology, scientists still have much to learn about twisters.

A big reason is that tornadoes are elusive. "They're small, they're rare, [and] they're very short-lived. If you see a tornado and decide you're going to drive towards it, often by the time you get there, it's over," Wurman says. Even if you get close to one, it is hard to tell what is going on inside it. "You can't go there. You can't see it."

Wurman knows the need for better tornado forecasting. On May 3, 1999, he found himself chasing tornadoes that threatened Norman, Oklahoma, where he lived—and where his wife and baby were at home.

His team was racing south through Oklahoma City toward Norman, following the storm. Recalling the scene as if it were happening, he says, "Pieces of wood

HOW TORNADOES FORM

A tornado is a violent, rotating column of air that reaches from a thunderstorm to the ground. Tornadoes can occur in many parts of the world, but they turn up most frequently in the United States, east of the Rocky Mountains, during the spring and summer months.

Before thunderstorms develop, a change in wind direction and speed starts air in the lower atmosphere spinning sideways, like a rolling log.

As the thunderstorm develops, rising air within it tilts up the rotating air. A rotating column of air 2 to 6 miles wide now extends through much of the storm. Most strong and violent tornadoes form within this area.[3]

and insulation and stuff are falling on the road, so we know it's chewing up homes. It's a very bad tornado. . . . It was heading towards Norman, and I was trying to call my wife and say, 'Get out of there.'"

The tornado missed his town, but Wurman recalls the path of destruction it left in Oklahoma City. "We were driving through neighborhoods that had been destroyed. It was pretty shocking. My memory of it is [that] everything was brown, because all this mud and dirt had been thrown around. Nobody was out there. Power poles were down. People had been killed. We

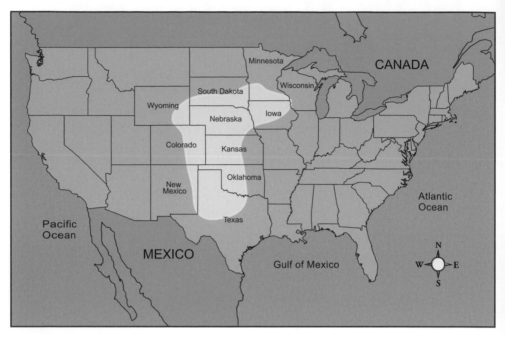

"Tornado Alley", the area of the United States where tornadoes are most frequent, is shown in yellow on this map.

had no idea what the scope of it was. We just kept driving. We were still going after the tornado. That was our job."

The Central Plains are prime hunting ground for tornadoes. A part of this region sees so many twisters that it is known as "Tornado Alley." This area includes parts of Texas, Oklahoma, Kansas, Nebraska, and other states. The land is basically flat, so cold, dry air from the north can meet warm, moist air from the Gulf of Mexico. Wurman says a third factor is air that flows off the Rocky Mountains and forms a cap that bottles up the energy in the air below it. When the cap can no longer contain that air, "there's so much energy it's almost explosive," he says. This is when storms are most likely to form tornadoes. These conditions are most common in the springtime.[4]

"There are other areas of the world that have tornadoes, but they tend to be less violent and much less frequent," Wurman says.

Hunting Tornadoes

Weather forecasters can predict when tornadoes are likely, but they still cannot say precisely when and where a twister will appear. When Wurman heads out for a day of tornado hunting, he knows he is likely to return empty-handed.

Batman has the Batmobile. Wurman has the DOW. That is short for Doppler on Wheels. The DOW is a truck equipped with a special kind of radar unit called a **Doppler radar** unit. By bouncing radio signals off raindrops, bugs, or dust suspended in wind, a Doppler radar unit can measure the wind's speed toward or away from the radar.[5]

A tornado expedition may last several days, with meals on the road and nights in motels. Wurman travels with a small support team in the DOW and

The Doppler on Wheels is equipped with a Doppler radar unit to measure the speed of the wind.

a sport utility vehicle. Wurman calls the SUV "a geekmobile" because it bristles with radio antennas and weather instruments. It is really the team's scout car. It can run ahead to check road conditions and find parking spaces for the truck, or it can dash close to a tornado, check air temperature and pressure near it, then speed away—something the truck, heavy with radar gear, can't do as well.

Some people have made a business of chasing storms. They lead tours across the plains, their customers hoping to glimpse a twister. Sometimes groups follow Wurman's hard-to-miss DOW. However, Wurman downplays the adventurous side of his work.

"I can't say it's exciting because we're so busy doing what we're doing. There's a lot of stress associated with picking the right part of the state, picking the right county, picking the right storm, getting on it at the right time, making the right road choices. Amateur chasers are probably having a lot more fun than I am when I'm leading the fleet out there."

Sometimes he gets excitement he could do without. Being pinned down in the 2004 thunderstorm was one of those times. He did not know it then, but the winds blowing around the tornado were fiercer than the funnel itself.

This is what the DOW looks like on the inside.

"We just turned the truck into the wind," he recalls. That made it the smallest possible target for flying debris—and the approaching twister. "The tornado got within half a mile of us and then turned in another direction. But we couldn't have done anything."

New Places to Explore: Inside Storms

Josh Wurman is a scientist, but he is also an explorer. "A hundred years ago, I'm sure I'd be on a boat, looking for new islands, or continents, or something," he says. "Sometimes I think it's a loss, but that sort of discovery is all done. There are no more continents, or islands, or rivers left to discover. There are still places to discover, going down into deep-sea trenches and places like that. . . . Inside tornadoes, inside hurricanes, places like that are among the last places to explore."

Wurman received a bachelor of science degree from the Massachusetts Institute of Technology (MIT) in 1982, but his interest turned to weather science. "Meteorology has some very big, interesting problems [that] you can see every day. What makes a tornado? What makes lightning? What causes climate change? All those things are very in-your-face

KILLER TORNADOES

The deadliest tornado in American history was the Tri-State Tornado of March 18, 1925. On that day, a single monster tornado tore across 219 miles of Missouri, southern Illinois, and southwest Indiana at freight-train speed, an average of 62 miles per hour. The twister was blamed for 695 deaths, more than 2,000 injuries, and the destruction of more than 15,000 homes.[6]

Sometimes a chain of storms will spin out many tornadoes across a large area. Scientists call it a tornado "outbreak." The tornado outbreak of April 3–4, 1974, was the worst outbreak in U.S. history. The National Oceanic and Atmospheric Administration calls it the "super tornado outbreak" as well as the "Xenia Tornado Outbreak," for the Ohio city where a monster tornado killed more than 30 people. In all, 148 twisters touched down in 13 states, killing 330 people and injuring 5,484.[7]

kinds of problems. My feeling was they can be tackled by mere mortals." He continued his studies at MIT to earn a master's degree and then a doctor of science degree in meteorology.

His first research job was with the National Center for Atmospheric Research (NCAR) in Boulder, Colorado. NCAR is a research center managed by the

University Corporation for Atmospheric Research. This is a group of more than one hundred universities that pool their research dollars to tackle projects that are too big for any one of them alone. NCAR also gets some research money from the federal government. In return, NCAR research helps the government learn better ways to predict dangerous weather.

It was at NCAR in 1994 that Wurman got the idea of putting a Doppler radar on a truck to chase down tornadoes. He started raising money and gathering hardware. He continued to work on it when he took a job as a professor at the University of Oklahoma in October 1994. He built a lot of it himself, with help from graduate students and his wife. He started using it the next spring.

Wurman still remembers the first time he aimed the DOW's radar antenna at a tornado. Suddenly, he was seeing the twister in "thousands of times" more detail than he had seen before. "I just remember looking at my [radar] screen, and I was just shocked. It was amazing."

Wurman says the DOW is "like having a new microscope. You look at pond water [with a microscope] and you see all the things in pond water. . . . Every place we look with these mobile radars, we see new

DOPPLER ON WHEELS

Mobile weather radars were a novelty when Dr. Josh Wurman built his first storm-chasing Doppler on Wheels in the mid-1990s. Since then, the number and types of mobile weather radar units have grown. Government agencies and universities around the country have mounted different kinds of radar units on trucks to study weather. Each one is a little different from the others, but they have the same basic parts: a flatbed truck; a radar antenna mounted on a turret, which allows an operator to turn or tilt the radar while the truck is moving or parked; and a box-shaped control cab that houses the radar's electronics, computers, and other gear.[8]

things, some of which we expected, some of which we don't understand."

Working in Weather Science

A weather scientist can expect to earn from $70,000 to $140,000 annually, according to the scientists interviewed for this book. Wurman also directs his own research center in Boulder. Its name is the Center for Severe Weather Research. He has a handful of employees and a small fleet of mobile radar units. He has used mobile radar units to study the winds in tornadoes, hurricanes, and wildfires across the United States and in Europe.

Wurman's center works closely with the National Center for Atmospheric Research. Much of the money for his research comes from the National Science Foundation, a federal agency that supports scientific research.

People in different careers support Wurman's research. For example, he works with an engineer who supplies weather equipment to scientists around the world, and he has worked with a filmmaker who made an IMAX film about tornadoes.

Wurman says few scientists are as independent as he is, but he likes the freedom to pursue his own ideas. "I guess I have a very determined streak," he says.

CHAPTER 3

Storm Peak Science

Anna Gannet Hallar is a weather scientist who straps on skis to get to work.

She is the director of the Storm Peak Laboratory in Colorado. It sits atop Mt. Werner on the Steamboat Springs Ski Resort. The lab is high—10,500 feet, or nearly two miles, above sea level. It is a third of a mile above the town of Steamboat Springs, where Hallar lives.

In the summer, Hallar may drive up the mountain in a sport utility vehicle or a "four-wheeler," an all-terrain vehicle. But in the winter, she typically uses skis and the resort's ski lifts to reach it.

"In the winter, I either drive or walk down to the ski resort and take the gondola [ski lift] to the top. Then, I have to ski down to catch another lift," she says.[1] She does this again to catch a third lift, which drops her off just a few feet from the lab.

The Storm Peak Lab overlooks a long slope almost bare of trees. It takes the brunt of every storm that hits the mountain. "We're extremely exposed, so we

Hallar and her husband, Ian McCubbin, on the roof of the Storm Peak Lab.

get pretty heavy storms," Hallar says. It gets windy, too. "It reached 100 miles per hour last winter, and we were worried about losing instruments. We get struck by lightning frequently and lose power."

While lightning might knock out electrical power to the lab, Hallar says the lab itself was built to protect its occupants. "We're extremely well grounded. There are lightning rods all over the place."

Working in a mountaintop lab in the middle of a storm might not be everyone's idea of a dream job. Hallar revels in raw weather. "We had a cool storm yesterday," she said in the summer of 2007. "It was hailing and lightning, and the wind was shaking the windows. And then we came outside, and there was a double rainbow."

Not All the Comforts of Home

The lab belongs to the Desert Research Institute, a part of the Nevada System of Higher Education.[2] It has rooms for laboratory work. It also has a full kitchen and two bunkrooms, with enough beds for nine people. With this setup, scientists can work for days at a time, a group of students can make an overnight visit, and anyone caught by a storm can ride it out safely.

Hallar and her husband sometimes use a four-wheeler to drive back and forth from the lab.

Both work and weather have kept Hallar in the lab overnight. "Some days we stay because we're studying the weather," she says. "[In winter] I'm normally working until it's dark and then skiing home in the dark, with headlamps. If it's blowing really hard, it isn't safe," because the blowing snow blocks the headlamps. When that is the case, she stays overnight. Her husband, Ian McCubbin, understands. He is also a scientist and the lab's site manager, which means he is responsible for repairs and supplies.

The lab has electricity, but not all the comforts of home. Hallar and her husband make a weekly supply run. In the winter, that can mean hauling supplies up the mountain on a snowmobile towing a sled. They melt snow to make water for drinking, cooking, and washing. The lab's two toilets do not flush. Hallar says they are "combustion toilets" that get rid of waste by burning it in a hot flame.

The lab is there for the same reason Hallar is. Its lofty perch exposes it to free-flowing air that has not mixed with nearby surface-level dust and chemicals. This is a layer of the atmosphere that scientists call the **free troposphere**. The lab is also in clouds much of the time, which allows Hallar and others to study clouds without leaving the ground.

Polluting Distant Skies

Hallar's specialty is atmospheric chemistry—measuring chemicals in the air. Chemicals can range from the natural gases that make up the atmosphere to water droplets in clouds and airborne pollutants from human activities.

"I study mainly pollution and how atmospheric pollution affects humans," she says. Her research helps scientists understand how pollution made in one place can become a problem far away.

For example, in 2006 and 2007, she took air samples that were found to contain traces of mercury.

The air currents were backtracked to show they had come from eastern Asia, halfway around the world. Mercury is a metal that can cause serious health problems in humans. The burning of coal in power plants can release mercury into the air. It can be a problem anywhere coal is burned, but Hallar's research showed that airborne mercury can drift deep into the United States from as far away as Asia.[3]

Science has been a lifelong pursuit for Hallar, who admits she likes to tinker with scientific instruments. "I was definitely interested in science my whole life, but I got more interested in physics in high school. In college, I did an internship with the National Weather Service, and that was a life-changing event."

Hallar grew up on a farm in central Missouri and attended Truman State University in Kirksville. During college, she received a summer internship at the National Weather Service's weather forecasting office in Pleasant Hill. The internship offered college credit, as if she were taking a course. Better yet, it let her sample different kinds of careers in weather science. "You got to do a little bit of everything," she recalls.

For example, she visited a local television station and watched a meteorologist work up the nightly weather report. She also took part in a program called SKY-WARN, which trains everyday people to become storm spotters for the Weather Service. What impressed Hallar most was her visit to an automated weather station. It sparked her interest in the makeup of Earth's atmosphere.[4]

After earning a bachelor's degree in physics from Truman, Hallar decided to study atmospheric science in graduate school. She earned a master's degree from the University of Colorado at Boulder in 2001 and a PhD from that same university in 2003.

Frigid Flight to Antarctica

Hallar's studies led her all the way to Antarctica. In 2002, while she was still a graduate student, she flew in a U.S. Air Force C-17 transport jet to **McMurdo Station**, the largest U.S. outpost on the continent.[5] She studied the breakdown of ozone in the air. Ozone is a natural chemical in the atmosphere that screens harmful ultraviolet rays from the sun. Scientists have found that certain manufactured chemicals in the air have weakened the ozone screen, especially over Antarctica.

Hallar was with a team of scientists studying how changes in sunlight affect ozone breakdown. The

STORM PEAK LABORATORY

Storm Peak Laboratory is located on Mount Werner at the top of the Steamboat Springs Ski Resort in Colorado. Its elevation is 10,500 feet above sea level. It was built there so scientists could study the atmosphere above the turbulent layer near the ground. It is also a teaching facility for students from grade school through college. Special facilities include a full kitchen and bunks for nine people, a cold room for studying snow and ice, a rooftop deck for air and cloud sampling, and a computer lab.[6]

team arrived in August, at the tail end of the Antarctic winter when the days were still dark. "It's the coldest time of the year, actually. It was like minus 50," she says. They stayed until the Antarctic summer season, when there is daylight at all hours.

McMurdo might be the biggest outpost in Antarctica, but it is still small and remote. About one thousand people work there in the Antarctic summer, and the population dwindles to about two-hundred and fifty in winter. The station depends on ships and airplanes for supplies.[7]

"I was considered extremely lucky because I had a vehicle assigned to me," she says. "I had a car . . .

because I had to go to a station outside of McMurdo, and I had to drive there." A typical work day for Hallar started by bundling up in warm layers covered by a parka, driving on a rough road of volcanic rock to the research station, then climbing onto its roof to melt ice off of weather instruments.

Sometimes she braved the cold just to escape the confines of McMurdo's cramped quarters. "You do need to get outside because you're there so long. I would take hikes and bundle up like crazy," she says.

Smog in Paradise

What's the opposite of Antarctica? Maybe the Maldives, a string of sunny coral islands in the Indian Ocean. Hallar went there in October of 2004 as a research associate for the National Aeronautics and Space Administration (NASA). She was part of an international study of air pollution.

Far from any mainland, the Maldives might be the last place you would think of to study air pollution, but Hallar said she found it there.

"It was a beautiful place and it was really nice," she says, but in October and November, air currents from India and Asia carry pollution across the northern islands. When that happens, she says, "[It's] like a smoggy day in Los Angeles. . . . It's kind of incredible."

Hallar's Maldives assignment came while she was working for NASA's Ames Research Center in northern California. She worked there from February of 2004 to July of 2006. NASA is known as America's space agency, but it also does a lot of research with airplanes. At Ames, Hallar worked on an instrument that was flown on NASA airplanes to study particles of pollution in the air. She didn't go on most flights, but it was her job to make sure the delicate instrument was working correctly. She also analyzed the data it collected.

Of the few research flights she has made, one during her college years stands out in her memory. In April of 2000, when she was a graduate student at the University of Colorado, she flew on a C-130 transport plane. The C-130 is a big plane with four propeller engines. The National Center for Atmospheric Research uses one for airborne research. Hallar went on a flight to study water vapor in the **boundary layer**. This is the layer of the atmosphere closest to the earth, and it can be bumpy. Hallar recalls climbing up to the cockpit for a pilot's eye view of the flight. She enjoyed it, but when she climbed

Some local schools send students on field trips to the lab. There, they conduct weather experiments with scientists like Hallar.

back down into the airplane's windowless cabin, the rocking and rolling motions made her sick. Since then, she has been happy to let her instruments do the flying without her.

In the Clouds but on the Ground

At Storm Peak Lab, Hallar can study clouds and air pollution without leaving the ground or going halfway around the world. She described the lab in a November 2006 interview with *Steamboat Today*, a local newspaper. "[The lab] allows us to do field research without having to travel. We can have a life. This is the perfect place," she said.[8]

Hallar also runs the lab's education program. She welcomes more than 1,000 students per year. Some are college students who come to do research. But some local schools send students as young as fifth grade up to the lab on field trips. Many start the trip in school buses, but they arrive just as Hallar does— on skis and ski lifts. During their trip, some students measure the air from town to the top of the mountain. It gives them a chance to see firsthand how air temperature and pressure change with altitude. At the lab, students can peer through microscopes at snowflakes in a room where the air is kept cold for snow and ice research.

Hallar says she enjoys the research she does. She especially likes coming up with an idea about the atmosphere and then thinking up experiments to test it. "The results I find incredibly rewarding," she says. She also enjoys teaching children about the lab and her work. She never knows which visit might spark an interest in some boy or girl to become a scientist like her.

CHAPTER 4

Alaska: Wild State, Wild Weather

Gary Hufford is a weather scientist in Alaska. When he goes out on the job, he often carries an unusual tool: a gun.

Hufford is the Alaskan region scientist for the National Weather Service. His office is in Anchorage, Alaska's biggest city. But Hufford's work often takes him out of the city,

35

Dr. Gary Hufford is the Alaskan region scientist for the National Weather Service.

and much of Alaska is wild. Big grizzly bears roam freely in many of the places he goes.[1] For safety, he carries a high-powered rifle or a beefy handgun.

"We're one of the few places where some of our [Weather Service] employees are trained to handle a weapon," he says.[2]

Weather research in Alaska is a big job. Alaska is the biggest state in the union: It is more than twice the size of Texas. Alaska's coastline, stretched out straight, could circle the earth twice. Its tallest mountain is nearly four miles high.[3] It lies farther north than any other state, and it stretches across the Arctic Circle.

Roads reach only a small part of the huge state. "It

means you do a lot of flying [to reach remote weather stations]," Hufford says. "Sometimes you have to go in by boat. To get to some of the sites, you have to do it in winter so you can land on skis on the snow. Other places you land on a local lake [in a plane equipped with floats] and hike over."

Getting to remote spots is not easy. Getting out is not always easy, either. Hufford recalls a visit he made to a Weather Service station in McGrath. It is a town of a few hundred people in south central Alaska. He flew there in a small, single-engine airplane. While he was there, the temperature fell to -72°F. The pilot

When traveling to remote locations, Hufford gets a bird's eye view of Alaska, like this one.

would not try to start the plane—much less fly it—for fear that the deep cold would damage the engine. "The rule among [Alaskan] pilots is that they will not fly if it's colder than minus forty," Hufford says. Below that temperature, he says, an airplane's fuel can start turning to jelly, and if an engine quits, it might not start again. Hufford had to wait six days until the severe cold eased.

A Little Warming, a Lot of Change

It is easy to see why weather forecasting in Alaska is tricky, but something unseen might be making it even trickier: **global warming**.

The earth's surface has warmed by about one degree Fahrenheit over the past one hundred years. The warming hasn't been the same everywhere, but on average the Arctic region has warmed almost twice as fast as other regions of the planet.[4]

Alaska is sensitive to climate change because much of it lies in a zone where a small change in temperature can have a big impact. "Unlike some places, where the difference between seventy-four degrees and eighty degrees may not mean much, two degrees here can cause great havoc," Hufford says. That is

WHAT IS GLOBAL WARMING?

Global warming is a rising trend in the average temperature of the earth's surface. Scientists agree that the earth's surface has gradually warmed in recent centuries, and the rate of warming has increased. As the earth warms, glaciers and polar ice sheets have been melting, and the global average sea level has been rising.

In 2007, a world panel of scientists said most of the global warming in the last half-century was very likely caused by humans—mainly from burning coal and oil, which puts carbon dioxide into the atmosphere. Carbon dioxide is what scientists call a **greenhouse gas** because it traps heat as a greenhouse does. The scientists predicted global warming will get worse if people do not reduce activities that make greenhouse gases, such as burning coal and oil.[5]

because temperatures across Alaska are often near the freezing point of water. A small change in temperature can mean the difference between frozen ground and mud, or between growing or shrinking **sea ice** along the coastline.

As temperatures have risen, Hufford has seen some big changes in Alaska's weather. For example, he says, bad storms on the Bering Sea are hitting the coastline more often. Ten storms socked the coast from 1980 to 1996. But a dozen storms hit in just the next eight years. The storms cause flooding and wash away land. Some villages along the coast could be wiped out by another bad storm, Hufford says.

Is the rash of storms caused by global warming? Is it a sign of things to come or just a short-term change? Hufford is trying to find out.

Weather and Climate

"In the Weather Service, our main . . . mission is saving lives and property," Hufford says. Accurate forecasts can help people avoid or prepare for bad weather.

To forecast the weather for a certain place, a weather forecaster needs to know how weather usually behaves there. If you know how it behaves, you are better able to predict what it's likely to do next when it begins to change. How weather behaves from year to year in a certain place is called its climate. The study of climates is called climatology.

"Am I going to forecast ninety [degrees] tomorrow for Anchorage when it's thirty today? Climatology tells me I don't see those kinds of temperatures," Hufford says.

But that approach does not work if the climate is changing. Weather might start following new patterns that forecasters do not know how to predict. "If the climate is changing, then all of a sudden I'm going to start having [forecasting] problems," Hufford says. Hufford says his research is aimed at learning how climate change affects short-term forecasts.

Hufford uses different methods to study Alaska's climate. For example, pictures from space satellites show how much of the ocean off Alaska's coastline is covered with ice. It is important to know where the edge of the ice is. It can affect ocean traffic, fishing boats, and coastal villages whose residents venture out on the ice to hunt and fish.

To measure sea ice, Hufford created a system for catching almost any kind of satellite picture. It snags pictures radioed down from satellites of different nations as they fly over Alaska. It is called the High Resolution Image Processing System, or HIPS. It gives Hufford many satellite pictures that show the sea ice around Alaska.

He says the satellite pictures show that Alaska's sea ice is shrinking—about 10 percent in area since the late 1970s. The sea ice also forms three weeks later in the year and melts three weeks sooner.

CLIMATE CHANGE IN ALASKA

The state of Alaska blames a host of growing problems on climate change. Its woes include melting glaciers, rising sea levels, and flooding of coastal communities. Warming of oceans and melting of land-based ice increase the volume of ocean water. Loss of sea ice cover changes the habitats of Arctic species and leaves coastal communities more exposed to larger waves generated by severe storms. More than 160 Alaskan coastal villages are threatened by coastline erosion. Three—Shishmaref, Kivalina, and Newtok—are making plans to move. Thawing permafrost—or ground that used to stay frozen year around—and more violent storms are damaging roads, utilities, pipelines, and buildings. Rising sea levels and changes in rain and snowfall will affect safe water sources in villages, contribute to the erosion of coastlines and riverbeds, and damage Alaska's vast forests. Changes that affect wildlife hurt native Alaskans' way of life, which depends on hunting and fishing. For example, the loss of coastal sea ice makes traditional hunting and fishing on the ice more difficult and dangerous. Alaska also has witnessed a record loss of forests to fires and spruce bark beetles, which have spread as the climate has warmed.[6]

Storms and Sea Ice

That sounds like a small, slow change. But Hufford says it is a big deal to people who live near the ocean. That's because the sea ice helps protect the coastline from damage caused by storms. "Sea ice acts like an extension of land. People living along the coast are no more affected [by storms] than if they lived inland. Without sea ice, storms build bigger waves, causing coastal flooding."

Combine the loss of sea ice with more frequent storms, and the impact of climate change becomes even more severe. Because of the flooding, the people of some coastal villages are trying to move their communities to new locations.[7]

Now, satellite data helps scientists like Hufford measure climate change. But the kind of satellite data Hufford uses has only been available since the 1970s. Even weather data taken on the ground in Alaska covers a relatively small range of years. To take the measure of a region's climate, scientists need to know the average of its weather over many decades. "That's a real challenge [in Alaska], because we're a young state," Hufford says. For example, he says regular weather observations for Anchorage did not begin until around 1920. That is a short time for gauging the climate, he says. "We simply don't have those long-term records that you find in other places."

Year by year, the Weather Service is building those records. It uses a network of small, ground-based weather stations with automated instruments to observe the weather across Alaska. It also has larger stations with weather observers scattered across the state. Part of Hufford's job is to find good spots for new weather stations and to check the stations from time to time.

Today's Forecast: Bear

Hufford says he does not go out alone because of the risk of bear attacks. Bears are less likely to attack a pair of people, and they are much less likely to attack a group of three, he says.

Some bears put this idea to the test in June of 2004. Hufford was leading a group of three people to check a site for a possible weather station. The site was at Cold Bay on the Alaskan Peninsula.

"We were out on Russell Creek. This is the only major salmon stream for many miles around. For that reason, it is not unusual to see half a dozen to a dozen brown bears fishing on any given day."

The scientists were studying the site and "not

Hufford ran into trouble with some Alaskan brown bears like these.

paying too much attention," Hufford admits, when a mother bear and two cubs burst out of a screen of bushes along the creek just a few dozen yards away. "This was too close an encounter, and she charged."

Hufford thought the bears were going to attack. "But as she charged us with her cubs, she got within about thirty feet, and she simply stopped and broke off and took off in another direction.

"Her cubs were so tied up on us they're still staring at us. They slow up a little bit, turn to look where mom is, and mom is gone. This is in June, and what was happening was [the mother bear] was dumping her cubs on us."

Hufford says the cubs were old enough to be on their own. He thinks their mother was looking for a chance to get away. "She wanted to get their attention on us while she took off."

Hufford's group froze, and waited to see if the cubs would keep charging. They were armed with a rifle and a handgun, but they did not want to shoot unless they had to.

"As soon as they realized Mom was gone, [the cubs] came to a total stop," Hufford says. "They spent two or three minutes wandering around trying to figure out what to do, then took off."

From River to Weather

The outdoors was always a part of Hufford's life. He lived along the McKenzie River near Eugene, Oregon. His father was a boat guide who took people on fishing trips. Those trips sparked Hufford's curiosity about water and weather. "I was real curious about the environment. When I got into high school, I had a teacher who was very influential who really encouraged me to go towards science."

The river steered Hufford towards oceanography—the study of the oceans. But he became interested in what happens where ocean and air meet. For example, heat and moisture from the ocean feed hurricanes. While studying ocean science, Hufford says, "I took so many meteorology courses, I qualified for a meteorologist." Attending Oregon State College, he earned a bachelor's degree in general science in 1964 and a master's degree in oceanography in 1967. He earned a PhD in oceanography from the University of Connecticut in 1978.

Hufford completed his doctorate with field research in Alaska. He is now a federal government employee. He says the government's salary range for his work is $50,000 to $90,000. He gets an extra 25 percent because his job is in Alaska, where living expenses are higher than the national average. But Hufford also went to Alaska because he loves the outdoors. Besides his science work, Hufford co-owns a fishing lodge and works part of the time as a fishing guide.

CHAPTER 5

Flying Through Hurricanes

When hurricanes pound America's coastlines, thousands of people flee inland to escape the dangerous winds and floods. Some scientists do just the opposite. They go right into the storm to study it. In 2005, Wen-Chau Lee flew through two of history's most destructive hurricanes. He was gathering new data to learn how such storms work.

Lee is a scientist with the National Center for Atmospheric Research in Boulder, Colorado. He studies hurricanes. His specialty is the use of airborne Doppler radars to observe winds inside hurricanes.

People have known and feared hurricanes for centuries. Modern weather forecasters track them with airplanes and satellites. But much about hurricanes remains a mystery, Lee says.

"We know the hurricane structure very well, especially in the mature stage," Lee says. "However, we still don't understand why and how it forms in the first place. . . . The process between a bunch of clouds over the ocean and how these clouds organize to form a vortex is unknown, not clear."

An airplane plowing through a hurricane can measure the speed, direction, temperature, pressure, and humidity of its swirling winds. But Lee says this gives data only along the line the plane flies through the storm. To get a better sense of what hurricanes are like, scientists blend data from many flights through many hurricanes.

But that, too, gives a fuzzy picture, Lee says. "It smooths the features out so you can get an idea of what hurricanes look like, but you cannot tell the character of an individual hurricane." He compares it

Dr. Wen-Chau Lee studies hurricanes using airborne Doppler radars.

to a person's picture taken with a low-quality digital camera. "You can sort of figure out that's a person, but you can hardly tell what that person looks like."

Lee is trying to sharpen our view of hurricanes. He uses Doppler radar to see into the heart of the storm. He says it's like using x-rays to see inside a human body. Although the Doppler radar uses radio waves instead of x-rays, "the radar can probe the internal structure of a hurricane," Lee says.

A Sharper View

It is not as easy as it sounds. Hurricanes usually form over the open ocean, far from land and ground-based radars. Some newer satellites use radio waves to probe hurricanes. But satellites are thousands of miles up in space, and they do not have powerful radars. Again, Lee compares them to a digital camera that takes fuzzy pictures. That is not all: In the past, it took two radars probing the same hurricane from different angles to get good measurements.

Lee solves both problems by taking radar units close to hurricanes in an airplane. In fact, he flies right into them!

Airplanes have been used to study hurricanes for many years. The Air Force Reserve's Hurricane

NOAA scientists such as Dr. Lee often use P-3 Orion aircraft like this one to study hurricanes.

Hunters squadron flies through hurricanes to measure and track them. The National Oceanic and Atmospheric Administration (NOAA) flies two types of airplanes through hurricanes to study them. They are Lockheed P-3 Orions. The Orion is the size of a small airliner. It has four propellers. It also has special equipment to gather data about a hurricane. In the tail of each plane is a Doppler radar. About fifteen people fly in an Orion on a hurricane mission. Lee has flown on several missions in the NOAA planes to probe hurricanes with radar.

His first hurricane flight was in 1995 to study Hurricane Luis over the Atlantic Ocean. He remembers it well because it was a night flight. Both of the Orion planes were in the hurricane. They were flying patterns that sliced through the center of the powerful storm. Around the center, called the eye, the circling winds had formed a tight wall of clouds called the **eyewall**. The eye itself was clear.

"The first time we entered the eye it was near midnight and there was a full moon," Lee recalls. The winds in the eyewall were strong but smooth, and the air in the eye itself was calm. "I remember the captain said, 'Okay, you guys have about five minutes

This Hurricane Hunter plane is flying past the eyewall of Hurricane Katrina.

HURRICANE FACTS

- The word *hurricane* comes from Hurican, the name of a mythical Caribbean god of evil.

- A hurricane is a large tropical storm with fast, spiraling winds. A tropical storm becomes known as a hurricane when its winds reach 74 miles per hour. Some hurricanes have had winds of nearly 200 miles per hour.

- Hurricanes gain energy from warm ocean waters. Evaporation from seawater makes them stronger.

- Hurricanes are dangerous because they can bring high winds, heavy rainfall, and large waves called a storm surge.

- As hurricanes move inland away from the ocean, they lose their source of energy and die.

- Hurricane season, the time of the year when hurricanes are most likely to form, is from June 1 through November 30.

- Typhoons are the same as hurricanes, except they happen in the western Pacific Ocean.[1]

to walk around before we reach the eyewall on the other side.'"

Lee took off his seat belt and went to a window. "I saw this beautiful full moon, and I could see a very pale color like silver on the inside of the eye. There were two aircraft in the storm, both NOAA P-3s, so I knew at that time there were about thirty people in there. No one else."

A scientist on a hurricane research flight doesn't fly the airplane. Each P-3 has two professional pilots who control the plane. But Lee says a scientist leads the mission and tells the pilots where to fly to get the best data—and how to avoid the most dangerous weather.

Lee flew on two missions into Hurricane Luis. Surprisingly, he says he didn't bounce around too badly. In part, he says, that's because the more powerful hurricanes tend to have smoother winds. But it is also because the scientist leading the mission was watching the screens of two radars: one in the tail that is used to collect data and one in the nose that is used to look ahead for dangerous **turbulence**. Lee says part of the lead scientist's job is to warn the pilots of rough air ahead so they can dodge it.

Lee did not lead the missions into Hurricane Luis, or the mission he flew into Hurricane Jeanne in 2004. "In these two hurricanes, my role was pretty much a passenger, an instrument operator. I did not have the responsibility to guide the aircraft," he says. Part of

Hurricane Katrina, seen here from space, was the third deadliest storm in U.S. history.

his job was to learn what hurricane flights were like so he could lead them later.

That happened in 2005, when Lee found himself guiding a P-3 Orion through two of the most dangerous storms ever to hit the United States: Hurricane Katrina and Hurricane Rita.

Inside Monster Storms

Scientists rate a hurricane's strength on a scale of one to five. Five is the strongest. A hurricane becomes a Category Five storm when its winds reach 156 miles per hour. It changes categories as it grows stronger or weaker. Katrina and Rita both reached Category Five at their peaks.

Katrina formed in late August of 2005 and swept across south Florida before growing into a Category Five storm over the Gulf of Mexico. Its winds weakened before it struck the coasts of Louisiana and Mississippi. But it drove ashore huge waves called a storm surge. It battered and flooded communities along the coast. Most media attention focused on flooded parts of New Orleans, but other towns also saw severe damage.

Rita followed in less than a month. After peaking at Category Five, it came ashore at the Texas-Louisiana border as a Category Three storm. More than 3 million people fled from its path. While powerful, it caused far less death and destruction than Katrina.[2]

It was the first time in recorded history that the Gulf of Mexico saw two Category Five hurricanes in the same season. And the hurricane doubleheader just happened to come while several U.S. laboratories were making a big effort to study the inner workings of hurricanes.

What the scientists wanted to study were the storm's eyewall—where a hurricane's winds are the fastest—and its **rain bands**. Rain bands are bands of heavy rain and wind that spiral outward from the storm's center. Scientists wanted to learn how the eyewall and the rain bands affected each other to change a storm's intensity.

Storm Secrets Revealed

This time, three Orion planes would fly through the hurricanes: NOAA's two P-3s and a Navy P-3 that carried a more powerful Doppler radar. Lee led the Navy plane's missions.

"I had to tell the pilot where to fly. That was quite a nerve-wracking experience," Lee recalls. "You really do not enjoy these flights. You are responsible not only for the [flight's] scientific success, but you're also responsible for the safety of the crew. If you tell the pilot to make the wrong turn, the outcome can be pretty bad."

Lee says the idea was to fly between the rain bands and probe them with the radar—but not to fly into the bands themselves. The rain and wind between the bands were bad enough, but inside them the storm could be dangerously rough. During the flights, Lee kept an eye on the nose radar's screen to watch for dangerous weather in their path. Sometimes he

HURRICANE CATEGORIES

The National Hurricane Center measures hurricane intensity using a scale called the Saffir-Simpson Hurricane Scale. A storm becomes a Category One hurricane when its winds reach 74 to 95 miles per hour. From 96 to 110 miles per hour, it is a Category Two storm. Category Three ranges from 111 to 130 miles per hour. Category Four storms have winds from 131 to 155 miles per hour, and storms with higher winds are Category Five—the highest category.

would have to tell the pilot to swerve around a dangerous patch of sky. "That [was] a very intense operation," he says.

No matter what, flying inside a hurricane isn't a smooth ride. Lee's airplane plowed through some rain bands to reach the parts of the storm where the team wanted to collect data. Lee says the airplane shook and lurched through updrafts and downdrafts, and the din of the storm came through the cabin walls. "You can hear the rain pounding on the fuselage [the airplane's body]. And occasionally when we penetrate the rain band or the eyewall, there is some large hail. You hear the ice [hitting] the fuselage."

As rough as it was, Lee said he never got airsick on a hurricane flight. "Each person's tolerance is different," he says.

But the missions were exciting because the radar on Lee's plane could see five times more detail than the radars on the other planes. It was as if Lee had suddenly switched to a better camera to take someone's picture. "You suddenly see a lot of detail of this person's face. . . . You start to see the eyes, the nose, the lips," he says.

The radar showed new details of eyewalls forming and changing. Lee's plane's radar caught two eyewalls in Rita—the one surrounding the eye and a new one that had formed from rain bands outside the inner eyewall. Scientists believe rain bands in a hurricane tighten to form a new eyewall, which chokes off and replaces the inner one. They call this process the **eyewall replacement cycle**. "Typically when the hurricane goes through this type of cycle, it intensifies. That's why we're so interested in capturing this process," Lee says.

Lee said the research adds to what we know about hurricanes and helps NOAA's National Hurricane Center make better forecasts. Forecasting what a

DEADLIEST U.S. HURRICANES

The deadliest hurricane to hit the United States was an unnamed storm that struck Galveston, Texas, in 1900. It killed 8,000 people. Another unnamed storm killed 2,500 people when it struck southeastern Florida in 1920. Hurricane Katrina, in 2005, was the third deadliest storm in U.S. history: it was blamed for 1,500 deaths.[3]

hurricane will do before it strikes land can save many lives.

Lee says seeing his research make a difference in forecasting is what makes his work rewarding. "When other scientists start to use your work . . . you know every time there's a hurricane your work is involved and affects the prediction that the hurricane center's making. That's quite satisfactory."

"No Shortage of Weather"

Lee was born in Taiwan, an island of East Asia. He remembers two books his father brought him when he was young. One was about weather, and the other was about insects. "I ended up looking at the weather book much, much more than I looked at the insect book," he says.

No wonder. Taiwan is less than 300 miles long, but **typhoons**—the western Pacific version of hurricanes—hit it 3.5 times per year on average, Lee says. "There's no shortage of weather there, so that just fascinated me."

He wanted to study atmospheric science in college, but his parents wanted him to study engineering. Lee says he listed engineering for both of his top two choices when he applied for college. He listed atmospheric science third. After taking a tough college entrance test—similar to tests U.S. students take before entering college—Lee was given his third choice. He earned a bachelor of science degree in atmospheric science from National Taiwan University in 1981.

Then he came to the United States to continue his studies. He earned a master's degree at the University of California in Los Angeles in 1985 and a doctorate there in 1988. In doing research for graduate studies, he focused on the use of Doppler radar for severe weather observation. He says he decided to specialize in hurricanes because he thought he might return to Taiwan to teach. But, Lee says, he stayed because the United States offered the best atmospheric research programs and facilities—and "the best opportunity for a young scientist to make a difference."

CHAPTER 6

Lightning's Shocking Secrets

A thunderstorm can be a hair-raising experience—sometimes even literally. Perhaps nobody knows this better than Dr. Earle Williams.

Williams is a senior research scientist for the Massachusetts Institute of Technology (MIT) in Boston. His specialty is lightning. Williams has observed thunderstorms

This picture was taken when Dr. Earle Williams and his daughter, Allegra, were hunting thunderstorms in Niger, Africa.

around the world. But one of his most vivid memories is of a storm over the Grand Canyon in Arizona.

He was not doing research. He was just visiting the canyon one day in 2000. As he watched a storm cloud building over the canyon, he noticed a group of excited tourists at a railing on the rim.

"They were all snapping pictures of one another. . . . When you looked closely, you'd see their hair stand up suddenly and then relax, and stand up and relax," Williams recalls.[1] The tourists were getting a "charge" out of the gathering storm. An **electrostatic charge**, to be precise.

The storm cloud was building up powerful electric charges. The base of the storm held a negative charge, and it was teasing up a positive charge in the ground below—and in the people who were standing on it. It is just like the static charge that shocks you when you touch a doorknob, but on a bigger and more dangerous scale.[2]

"The electrostatic field was influencing their hair, but they didn't know what was going on. They were just amused and taking pictures of one another," he recalls.

In fact, he says, they were close to becoming human lightning rods. Opposite electrical charges attract, and the positive charge in the ground was trying to join the negative charge in the sky. All that kept them apart was the air. If the charge in the cloud built up enough, it would overcome the gap like a giant spark plug. The result could be a sudden flash of lightning as the cloud discharged electrons to the ground—possibly right through the people!

"That's the kind of situation that is very dangerous, because you know there is a big [electrostatic] field in the ground. There's plenty of energy to carry the lightning from the cloud to the ground and kill somebody," Williams says.

Despite the danger, Williams says he walked down to the group to warn them. He discovered they were Japanese tourists who did not speak English. They could not understand him. But they were lucky; the storm hurled no lightning.

Nature's Light Show

A thunderstorm is nature's most dazzling light show. How clouds can build up the electricity to make lightning is one the great mysteries of weather. Both are reasons why scientists like Williams study lightning.

There are more down-to-earth reasons, too.

WHAT CAUSES LIGHTNING?

A thunderstorm starts to form when moist, unstable air near the ground is forced to rise. Sun-warmed ground can heat the air above it, starting an updraft. Or an approaching cold front can force warmer air to rise.

The rising air loses heat. Moisture in the air condenses, forming a tall cloud. Some moisture falls out as rain, causing a downdraft. Other moisture freezes to the surface of small airborne particles. This forms ice crystals, larger ice particles called graupel, and hail.

The ice particles ride in the updrafts and downdrafts, colliding and building up static electricity (electrons) in the storm cloud. The top of the cloud becomes positively charged, and the base of the cloud becomes negatively charged.

If the charges become great enough, electrons will leap across the gap to other clouds or to the ground, causing a lightning flash.

The lightning superheats the air around it, causing it to expand with a boom—the thunderclap.[3]

Lightning kills people and sparks forest fires. And it can strike in strange ways.

You might think the safest place to be in a thunderstorm is deep underground. But lightning, according to a federal government report, likely caused a deadly coal mine disaster in West Virginia. Twelve miners died in the Sago Mine after a pocket of methane gas exploded on January 2, 2006. It caved in the mine entrance and filled the tunnels with deadly fumes. Investigators believe a lightning strike on the surface sent an electric jolt through a cable that went into the mine, triggering a spark that ignited the gas.[4]

The odds that you will ever be hit by lightning are only one in 5,000, says the National Weather Service. Still, lightning kills an average of sixty-two people every year in the United States—as many as tornadoes kill.[5] Williams says better warnings could lower the death toll, but better warnings depend on a deeper understanding of how thunderstorms work.

Williams has studied lightning around the world, especially on land near the equator. He says tropical lands are the best breeding grounds for thunderstorms because they get warmer than other parts of the earth—much warmer than an ocean surface, which is why more thunderstorms form over land.

Allegra Williams uses a very sensitive light detection device that can detect the flash from a lightning strike 30 miles away during the middle of the day. This is used to measure average flash rate of a storm.

The hot ground warms the air above it and creates strong updrafts, a key ingredient in thunderstorms. The top three thunderstorm regions are equatorial Africa, South America, and an area of the western Pacific Ocean around Indonesia. Williams says the big thunderstorms in the midwestern United States match any in the world, but scientists study storms in the tropics because they can count on seeing one nearly every day.

Danger Outside the Cage

Studying lightning can be dangerous work, but Williams says there are ways to work safely. "I know lots of people who study lightning, but I've never heard of an injury or a hazard to anyone who's keenly interested in lightning," he says. "They know how to protect themselves."

Williams led a lightning research expedition to western Africa in 2006. The team set up a research station on flat desert land in Niger. They shipped their gear in trailer-sized metal containers. The containers became their research quarters. Williams says they made excellent lightning shelters. Any lightning that hit them would be conducted to the ground on the outer surface of the metal. Says Williams,

A long line of well-organized thunderstorm cells approach the MIT
radar run by Dr. Williams in Niamey, Niger.

"Every facility I've worked in is basically a metal enclosure of some sort, which is very good protection against lightning."

Metal enclosures made for this purpose are called **Faraday cages**. They are named after British physicist Michael Faraday, a pioneer in the understanding of electricity. Williams says a metal car can act as a Faraday cage to protect its occupants in an electrical storm. But a car is not a perfect enclosure, as he saw firsthand.

"I remember one time driving along a highway in Orlando, Florida, in a big thunderstorm. There was a lightning flash to a road marker just to the left of my vehicle, probably within three feet of me. And I could feel it. . . . I could feel the electrostatic effects." Williams says the window in the car door made a big enough gap for a bit of the charge to reach him. "That's an example of having a Faraday cage with a hole in it."

That was not his only close encounter with lightning, but none have occurred while he was studying lightning. Williams says even on a research trip, his only close brush came when he was taking a break from his work.

That happened on a research project in northern

Australia near Darwin. Williams's family accompanied him on the trip, and he took them sightseeing one weekend. Along came what Williams calls a "runaway thunderstorm." It is called that because its lightning flashes nonstop. "This one was a very spectacular one, and the storm came right overhead, and the lightning hit a TV mast and blew sparks all over the place. . . . That one really got my attention."

Globe–circling Circuit

Williams does some of his worldwide research without leaving the United States. He can monitor thunderstorms around the world at a single station in Rhode Island. Its main instrument is a big metal ball on a pole.

Earth has what Williams calls a **global circuit**. The upper atmosphere carries a positive charge, while Earth's surface has a negative charge. The gap between those charged layers forms what Williams calls a waveguide, a zone in which a pulse of electromagnetic energy sends waves of a certain frequency all the way around the planet.

When a thunderstorm fires up somewhere on Earth, each lightning flash sends out these waves. A strong storm with lots of flashes generates waves

LIGHTNING FACTS AND SAFETY TIPS

- The United States sees about 25 million lightning flashes each year.

- Lightning has caused an average of 62 deaths per year for the past 30 years. An average of 300 lightning-related injuries are reported each year, but the National Weather Service thinks some cases go unreported, so the actual number is likely higher.[6]

- Lightning can strike as far as ten miles from where it is raining. That is about how far the sound of thunder travels. If you can hear thunder, you are within striking distance of lightning. Seek safe shelter immediately.

- Most lightning deaths and injuries occur in the summer. The National Weather Service urges that outdoor sport activities should stop at the first roar of thunder to give everyone time to get into a large building or enclosed vehicle.

- Indoors during a storm, do not use corded telephones, computers, or other devices with electrical cords. Stay away from pools, tubs, showers, and other plumbing.

- Wait 30 minutes after the last clap of thunder before going outdoors again.[7]

strong enough to be detected by the instrument in Rhode Island. The instrument allows scientists like Williams to measure daily thunderstorm activity around the planet.

Why bother? Williams says daily thunderstorm activity around the world might hold clues to global climate change. He said he began thinking about the link on his trips to the tropics. In observing the lightning closely, he noticed that when the temperature rose slightly, there was more lightning. When the temperature dropped, so did the lightning activity, Williams wonders whether the entire planet will respond in the same way as smaller regions do. Will a warmer Earth mean more lightning-producing storms?

Williams says scientists do not know how global warming affects thunderstorm activity worldwide. But keeping track of thunderstorms worldwide over many years will help scientists learn more about both global warming and thunderstorms.

From Science to Thunderstorms

Williams thinks where he lived when he was young had a lot to do with his interest in thunderstorms. He was born in South Bend, Indiana, and lived for twenty years in Culver, Indiana, about forty miles from South Bend. "There are great storms coming through there, really blockbusters," he says.

He also thinks his father had a big influence on him. "He was an artist, a sculptor, but he was also a telescope maker, and he had a broad range of [scientific] interests."

In college, Williams did not set out to study lightning. He studied physics and electromagnetic energy. He soon became fascinated with the physics of lightning. "It was really lightning that drew me into studying storms," he says. "Once I was interested in lightning, I needed to learn meteorology." Meteorology helped him understand how thunderstorms form in the first place.

Williams earned a bachelor's degree in physics from Swarthmore College in Swarthmore, Pennsylvania, in 1974. He earned a PhD in geophysics from MIT in 1981. Williams says a scientist on his level may earn approximately $80,000 to $160,000, depending on whether they choose to teach. He says he could earn more by working as a scientist for a private company. "But then you lose the freedom to do what you want to do," he says.

CHAPTER 7

Science on Sea Ice

North of Alaska and Canada's Northwest Territories, the vast and lonely **Beaufort Sea** stretches toward the North Pole. The Beaufort Sea is a part of the Arctic Ocean. Much of it is cloaked in ice throughout the year. Winters are dark and flesh-freezing cold. Even summer days can see snow or freezing rain. It is region visited by whales, seals,

Dr. Jennifer Katy Hutchings specializes in sea ice.

and polar bears—and scientists like Jennifer Katy Hutchings.

Hutchings is a British physicist at the University of Alaska in Fairbanks. She works in the university's International Arctic Research Center. Her research specialty is sea ice. Like many other scientists, she uses high-tech tools in her work. For example, data from space satellites helps her gauge the extent and thickness of sea ice. But satellites cannot tell her everything. To understand sea ice, she needs to go out on the ice itself. For several years, she has been doing just that, sometimes twice a year. It is hard, dangerous work.[1]

Scientists have been paying close attention to Arctic sea ice. Ice covers much of the Arctic Ocean year round in a great mass called an ice pack. At its winter peak, it covers some 6 million square miles—an area nearly twice the size of the United States.[2] But more of it has been melting in the summer. Scientists have noticed the ice beginning to melt earlier in the year and forming later.[3]

The Arctic Ocean's shrinking ice pack is one of many clues scientists have found that the earth's surface is getting warmer. But sea ice is not simple, like ice on a lake. It is a vast mass of frozen water that lies between the ocean and the air, so it affects how heat moves from one to the other. It even has an impact on how heat circulates through the world's oceans. Its annual cycle of forming and melting plays a complex role in Earth's climate. It is a role scientists are trying hard to understand.[4]

No Solid Ground

In winter, the Arctic ice pack is so big it looks like another continent. And it is so massive, it gives no

SEA ICE BASICS

Sea ice is frozen ocean water. It forms and melts in the ocean. It is not made of snow, but it usually becomes covered with snow.

More sea ice remains through summer in the Arctic than in the Antarctic. A big reason for this is that land nearly surrounds the Arctic Ocean, so the ice cannot easily drift off to other oceans. Ice also tends to become trapped in a swirling pattern of surface water called the **Beaufort Gyre**. Ice floes drifting in the gyre may stay frozen for several years and bump into other floes, forming thick pack ice.

The year-round Arctic ice pack has been measured at around two million square miles. At the end of winter, the ice pack covers about 6 million square miles.

As huge as the Arctic ice pack is, scientists say more of it melts every summer because of global warming; if the trend continues, they say, summers on the Arctic Ocean could become ice-free.[5]

hint that it is floating. "You really feel like you're on solid ground," says Hutchings.

But it is not solid. Tides, ocean currents, and storms push the sea ice around. Hutchings says the ice pack is a collection of huge pieces of sea ice that are constantly smashing together, grinding, and cracking. A crack can split the ice for miles, exposing stretches of open water called **leads** (pronounced

LEEDS). The exposed water gives up heat to the air and forms new ice. If the lead stays open, the new ice will thicken. If it closes, it will crumple the new ice into jagged ridges. The ridges may be several yards high and dozens of yards deep. All of this affects how much ice forms and how much lasts through the summer.

Hutchings focuses her research on the forces that move and reshape sea ice. She wants to understand how those forces affect ice formation. She uses her knowledge in working with other scientists to develop computer programs to predict changes in the Arctic ice pack. She hopes her research will improve our understanding of Earth's climate and the forces that affect it.

Studying sea ice is difficult and expensive. The Beaufort Sea is remote, and conditions are harsh. Research projects are usually joint efforts of government agencies and universities. Many projects involve more than one country.

Hutchings likes to go out on the Beaufort ice at the end of winter, when the ice pack is at its peak, and at the end of summer, at its low point. "[These are] the two periods when you can [best] compare the ice," she says.

Breaking the Ice—with a Ship

Her summer visits are between late July and early September. She travels on an icebreaker. An icebreaker is a powerful ship with a hull built strong for smashing through ice. The icebreaker is almost always on the move, so Hutchings sees much more sea ice on the cruises than she does at the winter ice camps. The Arctic summer has twenty-four hours of daylight, so scientists are at work around the clock.

What is the weather like on an Arctic cruise? "It feels like winter because the ice is everywhere and it's cold. But from my perspective, being there in the summer is rather nice," Hutchings says. That's because it is far warmer than in winter, when she visits the ice camps. On the summer cruises, "You don't have to worry about how many layers of gloves you want to wear and how you're going to write in your notebook when [the wind is blowing] outside." But it is often foggy, she says. That is because the ocean releases moisture into the chilly air. The moisture quickly condenses into clouds of tiny water droplets, forming a fog that can blanket the sea.

In summer, the southern Beaufort Sea looks like a jigsaw puzzle coming apart as the ice pack breaks up. The ice pieces are called **floes**. The icebreaker

An icebreaker is a ship with a strong hull for smashing through ice. On the ice, Hutchings and her colleagues are taking and testing samples.

weaves between the floes or smashes through them. Sometimes it stops at a floe so scientists can set up a station to study it more closely.

Hutchings relishes these stops. "I love being out on the ice. It's so special. It's a different world. It's almost like being on the moon sometimes, because it's so alien. It's a very peaceful environment," she says. In contrast, "The ship is noisy all the time."

In the summer of 2007, Hutchings traveled on the Canadian Coast Guard icebreaker *Louis S. St-Laurent*. It carried fifty-one crewmembers; twenty-seven scientists from the United States, Canada, and Japan; and a Japanese news team.[6] Most of the scientists were working on a project to study the water in the Beaufort Sea. But Hutchings and one of her students, Alice Orlich, were on the cruise to study the ice. The two worked in shifts; while one slept, the other made hourly observations of the thickness and condition of the **pack ice**.

A Seabird's Eye View

It was an especially exciting cruise for Hutchings. She flew over the sea in a helicopter launched from the ship. The ship uses the helicopter to scout the easiest path through the floes. Scientists use it to scout for

When they find a site that might be good for a station, scientists land a helicopter on the ice and check out the site.

good places to set up ice stations. Hutchings flew along as an ice station scout. The flights also gave her a bird's eye view of the ice she was studying.

The back of the ship has a landing deck for the helicopter. "It's quite exciting actually, taking off and landing from the ship," Hutchings says.

But flying over an icy ocean, far from ship and shore, has its risks. Hutchings says her flights ranged up to one hundred miles from the ship. Before flying, she took a survival course to learn how to get out of the helicopter if it went into the ocean.

"We dress warm, and we wear a life jacket that can be inflated outside of the helicopter," she says. "But it's not something I worry about too much because when we're traveling up there, there's ice around for the helicopter to land on. So if we're in trouble, the helicopter would land on the ice, and then we'd have to wait for the ship to come and get us." Pushing through the ice, the ship could take a couple of days to reach them, she admits. That is why the helicopter carries survival gear. "We are very alone up there. We're completely dependent on ourselves."

When the scientists spot a good site for a station, they land to check it out, then return to the ship. The ship plows its way to the site. But the scientists do not just jump onto the floe, Hutchings says. The deck is 30 feet or more above the surface of the ice. For safety, the ship lowers and lifts people onto and off the floe with a boxlike basket attached to a crane.

Among other things, scientists drill holes through the floe to measure its thickness. A floe can be several yards thick. They also drill out long, four-inch-wide rods of ice called cores. By measuring the saltiness and temperature of the core at different points,

By comparing ice core data with measurements from previous years, Hutchings can detect changes in temperature.

Hutchings says she can learn how old the ice is and how quickly it has been melting. By comparing the data with core measurements from the year before, she can tell whether the current summer has been warmer or cooler.

Off to Winter Camp

Winter visits are much different. In midwinter, the University of Washington's Applied Physics

Laboratory sends a team in a small airplane over the Beaufort ice pack to find a campsite. "They want to find a nice, strong piece of ice that's very old to put the camp on. Next to it they need to find a piece of very new ice that's flat," Hutchings says. The flat ice is needed for a runway, so a plane can land with building materials for a cluster of huts and fly in scientists and supplies.

The camp is built for the U.S. Navy, which does its own Arctic research for military purposes. The camp is set to house up to sixty Navy researchers. After the Navy has used the camp for several weeks, it allows other research groups to use it. Hutchings says about thirty scientists occupy the camp when she is there, along with seven support workers who cook, maintain the camp, and do other support work. At the end of winter, the camp is taken apart and flown back to land.

Late winter is bitterly cold with little daylight, Hutchings says. But the days lengthen rapidly around the spring **equinox** in March. An equinox is a moment when the sun is directly aligned with the earth's equator. On an equinox day, everywhere in the world sees nearly the same amount of daylight and darkness. "That far north, when you go through the equinox, you go very quickly from very long nights to very long days," she says. The reverse happens around the fall equinox.

The camp is not fancy. The huts are insulated but plain. They are heated with small oil stoves. Ice must be melted to make water for drinking and washing. And everyone must keep an eye out for polar bears. Hutchings says she has not seen a bear at an ice camp, but she has seen their tracks. Away from camp, people travel in groups for safety. They carry a flare gun to scare off an approaching bear and a rifle in case of an attack. Hutchings says it would take a well-aimed shot to stop a polar bear and she would not shoot one unless her life was at stake.

Her visits only last about two weeks. Like many other scientists, she works long hours to make the most of her time there. It is just as well, she says. It keeps her mind off the rough living conditions. "You're working so hard, you don't realize how rough it is. . . . You don't spend much time in your quarters. And we would be out up to 10 or 12 hours a day in the field. It's very intense."

Hutchings' specialty is studying the motions of the ice pack. For example, in 2006 she set up special instruments in different places on the ice. Each

HOW SEA ICE AFFECTS CLIMATE

Sea ice keeps the Arctic region cooler by reflecting sunlight back into space. Its bright surface reflects 80 percent of the sunlight that strikes it. In contrast, ocean water soaks up 90 percent of the sunlight that strikes it.

As saltwater freezes, the salt goes out of it. The water around it gets saltier and denser, so it sinks. The cold, dense polar water moves along the ocean bottom toward the equator, while warmer water above it moves toward the poles. Scientists call this circulation a "conveyor belt" that helps regulate global temperatures.

Sea ice forms a layer between water and air. It slows the transfer of heat from the ocean into the atmosphere. This results in lower air temperatures in the polar regions. Hutchings says the big difference in temperatures between the cold polar regions and the warm tropics is largely responsible for the weather patterns in North America. Changes in polar temperatures could change these patterns "dramatically," she says.

Storms, tides, and other forces put sea ice under stress and cause violent cracking. The cracks expose open water to the polar air. This allows heat to escape into the air. If the cracks stay open, new ice will form. If they close, they may form thick ridges of ice. Hutchings wants to know if changes in weather patterns on the Beaufort Sea will cause more cracks and ridges and whether the result will be more or less ice. She says this knowledge could help scientists predict how quickly a warming world might cause the summer ice pack to disappear.[7]

Cracks in the Arctic sea ice allow heat to escape into the air. Scientists like Hutchings are studying how this can affect global climate.

instrument uses satellite signals to measure the exact location of the ice. Each one also has a satellite telephone link to a University of Alaska computer. Every day, each instrument calls in its location from the distant pack ice. Hutchings has been using the instruments to track the movement of the pack ice.

A Dangerous Dip

In winter, it is easy to forget the thick pack ice is not solid ground—too easy, sometimes. In 2003, Hutchings nearly lost her life when she was literally driven through the ice into the ocean.

Hutchings was conducting an experiment to measure the opening and closing of leads, the patches of ocean that open up when pack ice cracks. A lead opened half a mile from the camp, and she set up instruments around it that used satellite signals to measure their locations as the crack widened and narrowed.

But another lead almost did her in.

Hutchings says she was riding on the back of a snowmobile. "The driver decided that the flat ice on the lead in front of us would be very nice to travel on," Hutchings recalls. She says she had warned the driver earlier that lead ice was often thin and unsafe.

The driver headed for it anyway. The surface of the lead ice was about a foot lower than the pack ice. The snowmobile, a heavy-duty machine, dropped onto the lead ice and broke through. The sled it was pulling went in with it.

"The next thing I knew, I was up to my waist in water, and then, I remember, the snow machine was sinking down underneath me. I grabbed hold of the sled . . . and then the sled was sinking, and I couldn't hold onto it any more." Hutchings grabbed the edge of the pack ice, but it was a foot above the water and slippery. "A lot of people who fall in leads often don't get out because you can't pull yourself out," she says.

That is another reason why people in ice camps travel in groups. Two other scientists were with them on another snowmobile, and they quickly pulled out Hutchings and the driver. They were two miles from camp, and Hutchings' heavy snowsuit was soaked. But she says the outer layer froze and blocked the wind, so she stayed warm inside until she could get into her hut and put on dry clothes.

Hutchings went right on with her work, but she admits the experience was scary. "After that, I went out into the field only when I absolutely had to. I was quite shook up, actually. I had nightmares that there would be a lead opening up underneath the camp."

Hutchings says accidents like hers are rare, and she has continued to go to the ice camps. But she says she learned a valuable lesson: Choose a field companion who cares about safety, accepts advice, and watches out for others.

A Life-changing Ship

Hutchings' interest in science is not surprising. Her father is a chemist. But her interest in sea ice was sparked at age eight by her visit to a ship: *Discovery*, the sailing ship used by British explorer Robert Falcon Scott to reach Antarctica in 1902. "It was moored in London and my mother took me to see it," she remembers. "Then I started reading about Captain Scott and Amundsen and their race to the South Pole." Norwegian polar explorer Roald Amundsen led the first successful expedition to the South Pole, reaching it in 1911. Scott reached it in 1912, but he and his four companions died on their return trip. Tales of their Polar journeys fascinated Hutchings. "Ever since then, I've been fascinated by the South Pole and Antarctica and the polar regions," she says.

She decided the best way to reach Antarctica was to

become a scientist and go there for research. In college, she chose to study physics. "It was such a broad subject that I thought it would give you the tools you need to understand anything in the world." But her work took her to the top of the world, not the bottom. After earning a bachelor of science degree in physics at the University College in London in 1995, she was offered a chance to work on her doctorate with someone who studied sea ice. This sparked an interest in the Arctic region that has become the focus of her work. "I've never got to Antarctica," she says with a laugh. She received a PhD in physics from the University College in London in 1999.

At the time this book was written, Hutchings was a postdoctoral research fellow. That means she was just starting her career as a scientist. She says people in her position earn between $35,000 and $50,000 per year.

While the work sounds adventurous, Hutchings says adventure is not what drives her interest. She spends most of the year in an office, analyzing data, writing reports, and seeking grants for new research projects. Hutchings says she enjoys thinking of questions about sea ice, such as why some leads close and form ridges while others stay open and grow new pack ice.

"I really enjoy answering that question and coming to an understanding of it," she says. "It's also very satisfying to realize that [with] each small step you make, and each small question you answer, you're enhancing all of humanity's understanding of how the climate works. And it might be a very small step, but I think it's always important."

Appendix:
Careers in Storm Science

Scientist	Title	Education	Average Salary
Joshua Wurman	Director, Center for Severe Weather Research	Bachelor's degree in physics, master's degree and ScD (doctor of science degree) in meteorology	$55,530 to $96,490
Anna Gannet Hallar	Assistant Research Professor and Director, Storm Peak Laboratory	Bachelor's degree in physics, master's degree and PhD in Atmospheric and Oceanic Sciences	$55,530 to $96,490 (meteorologist); $39,610 to $80,390 (professor)
Gary Hufford	Alaskan Region Scientist for the National Weather Service	Bachelor's degree in general science, master's degree and PhD in oceanography	$50,000 to $90,000
Wen-Chau Lee	Scientist, National Center for Atmospheric Research	Bachelor's degree, master's degree, and PhD in atmospheric science	$55,530 to $96,490
Earle Williams	Senior Research Scientist	Bachelor's degree in physics, PhD in geophysics	$80,000 to $160,000 (depending on teaching status)
Jennifer Katy Hutchings	Physicist, Postdoctoral Research Fellow	Bachelor's degree and PhD in physics	$35,000 to $50,000

Chapter Notes

Chapter 1. The Quest for Knowledge

1. Personal interview with Joshua Wurman, January 25, 2007. Unless otherwise noted, all quotes from Wurman come from this interview.

Chapter 2. The Fury of a Twister

1. Personal interview with Joshua Wurman, January 25, 2007.

2. National Weather Service Forecast Office, Norman, OK, "The Historic Forecast," December 28, 2007, <http://www.srh.noaa. gov/oun/tornadodata/firstforecast/> (March 4, 2007).

3. National Oceanic and Atmospheric Administration, "Tornadoes . . . . Nature's Most Violent Storms," September 1992, <http:// www.nssl.noaa.gov/edu/safety/tornadoguide.html> (March 4, 2007).

4. Personal interview with Joshua Wurman, and Windows to the Universe, "What is Tornado Alley?" *University Corporation for Atmospheric Research*, September 2000, <http://www. windows.ucar.edu/tour/link=/earth/Atmosphere/tornado/alley. html&edu=mid> (March 7, 2007).

5. National Weather Service, "Doppler Radar: Introduction," *Jetstream*, February 1, 2006, <http://www.srh.noaa.gov/srh/ jetstream/doppler/doppler_intro.htm> (March 7, 2007).

6. National Oceanic and Atmospheric Administration, "Remembering the March 18, 1925 Tri-State Tornado," n.d.,

<http://www.noaanews.noaa.gov/stories/s393.htm> (July 4, 2008).

7. National Oceanic and Atmospheric Administration, "1974 Tornado Outbreak," April 1999, <http://www.publicaffairs. noaa.gov/storms/> (March 7, 2007).

8. University Corporation for Atmospheric Research, "The Road to Doppler Data," *UCAR Quarterly*, Summer 2003, <http:// www.ucar.edu/communications/quarterly/summer03/doppler. html> (March 8, 2007).

Chapter 3. Storm Peak Science

1. Personal interview with Anna Gannet Hallar, September 6, 2007. Unless otherwise noted, all quotes from Hallar come from this interview.

2. Desert Research Institute Division of Atmospheric Sciences, "Welcome to the Desert Research Institute's Storm Peak Laboratory," *Storm Peak Laboratory*, 2007, <http://stormpeak. dri.edu> (October 9, 2007).

3. D. Obrist, A.G. Hallar, and I. McCubbin, "Mercury Monitoring at Storm Peak Laboratory in Colorado to Determine Regional and Asian Long-range Transport Contributions to Atmospheric Mercury Loads," presented at the International Conference on Air Quality, Arlington, VA, September 2007, abstract via e-mail from Hallar, October 10, 2007.

4. Anna Gannet Hallar, "Reflections on my Undergraduate Internship Opportunity," *Internships: A Taste of the Working*

World, Truman State University Career Center, April 9, 2003, <http://career.truman.edu/student/internship/hallar.asp> (October 11, 2007).

5. National Science Foundation, Office of Polar Programs, "McMurdo Station," December 12, 2006, <http://www.nsf.gov/od/opp/support/mcmurdo.jsp> (October 10, 2007).

6. Desert Research Institute Division of Atmospheric Sciences, Storm Peak Laboratory, "Facility Description," 2007, <http://stormpeak.dri.edu/site.html> (October 9, 2007).

7. National Science Foundation, Office of Polar Programs, "Your Stay at McMurdo Station Antarctica," NASA Quest, n.d., <http://quest.nasa.gov/antarctica/background/NSF/mc-stay.html> (October 11, 2007).

8. Melinda Mawdsley, "Office with a View: New Scientists Take Over Operation of Storm Peak Laboratory," *Steamboat Pilot & Today*, November 24, 2006, <http://www.steamboatpilot.com/news/2006/nov/24/office_view/> (October 15, 2007).

Chapter 4. Alaska: Wild State, Wild Weather

1. Alaska Department of Fish and Game, "Brown Bear," September 7, 2007, <http://www.adfg.state.ak.us/pubs/notebook/biggame/brnbear.php> (November 14, 2007).

2. Personal interview with Gary Hufford, March 22, 2007. Unless otherwise noted, all quotes from Hufford come from this interview.

3. University of Alaska Fairbanks, "Frequently Asked Questions about Alaska," Statewide Library Electronic Doorway, September 27, 2001, <http://sled.alaska.edu/akfaq/akgeogr.html> (April 1, 2007).

4. Intergovernmental Panel on Climate Change, *Synthesis Report*, November 2007, p. 8, <http://www.ipcc.ch/pdf/assessment-report/ar4/syr/ar4_syr.pdf > (July 2, 2008).

5. Intergovernmental Panel on Climate Change, "Summary for Policymakers," *Climate Change 2007: The Physical Science Basis*, Paris, February 5, 2007, <http://www.ipcc.ch/SPM2feb07.pdf> (April 16, 2007).

6. State of Alaska, "What will Climate Change Mean to Alaska?" *Alaska Climate Change Strategy*, n.d., <http://www.climatechange.alaska.gov/> (November 14, 2007).

7. State of Alaska, "What Will Climate Change Mean to Alaska?" *Alaska Climate Change Strategy*, n.d., <http://www.climatechange.alaska.gov/> (November 14, 2007).

Chapter 5. Flying Through Hurricanes

1. Atlantic Oceanographic and Meteorological Laboratory, Hurricane Research Division, "Frequently Asked Questions," October 19, 2005, <http://www.aoml.noaa.gov/hrd/tcfaq/A1.html> (April 23, 2007).

2. National Climatic Data Center, "Climate of 2005: Summary of Hurricane Rita," September 22, 2005, <http://www.ncdc.noaa.gov/oa/climate/research/2005/rita.html> (April 23, 2007).

3. National Weather Service, NOAA Technical Memorandum NWS TPC-5, "The Deadliest, Costliest and Most Intense United States Tropical Cyclones from 1851 to 2006," April 2007, <http://www.nhc.noaa.gov/Deadliest_Costliest.shtml> (April 25, 2007).

Chapter 6. Lightning's Shocking Secrets

1. Personal interview with Earle Williams, April 4, 2007. Unless otherwise noted, all quotes from Williams come from this interview.

2. NOAA, National Severe Storms Laboratory, "Lightning Basics," January 22, 2007, <http://www.nssl.noaa.gov/primer/lightning/ltg_basics.html> (May 10, 2007).

3. University Center for Atmospheric Research, "Lightning: Just for Kids," April 4, 2000, <http://www.ucar.edu/communications/infopack/lightning/kids.html> (May 19, 2007).

4. U.S. Department of Labor, Mine Safety and Health Administration, "Report of Investigation: Fatal Underground Coal Mine Explosion," May 9, 2007, <http://www.msha.gov/Fatals/2006/Sago/sagoreport.asp> (May 10, 2007).

5. National Weather Service, "Lightning—The Underrated Killer," *Lightning Safety*, n.d., <http://www.lightningsafety.noaa.gov/overview.htm> (May 10, 2007).

6. National Weather Service.

7. Ibid.

Chapter 7. Science on Sea Ice

1. Personal interview with Jennifer Hutchings, October 18, 2007. Unless otherwise noted, all quotes from Hutchings come from this interview.

2. National Atlas of the United States, "Profile of the People and Land of the United States," October 2, 2007, <http://nationalatlas.gov/articles/mapping/a_general.html> (November 15, 2007).

3. National Snow and Ice Data Center, "Arctic Sea Ice Shatters All Previous Record Lows," Press Release, October 1, 2007, <http://nsidc.org/news/press/2007_seaiceminimum/20071001_pressrelease.html> (October 30, 2007).

4. K.E. Trenberth and P.D. Jones, P. Ambenje, R. Bojariu, D. Easterling, A. Klein Tank, D. Parker, F. Rahimzadeh, J.A. Renwick, M. Rusticucci, B. Soden, and P. Zhai, "Observations: Surface and Atmospheric Climate Change," *Climate Change 2007: The Physical Science Basis, Contribution of Working Group I to the Fourth Assessment Report of the Intergovernmental Panel on Climate Change*, Cambridge University Press, n.d., p. 239, <http://ipcc-wg1.ucar.edu/wg1/Report/AR4WG1_Print_Ch03.pdf> (October 30, 2007).

5. National Snow and Ice Data Center, "Introduction," *All About Sea Ice*, n.d., <http://nsidc.org/seaice/intro.html> (November 8, 2007).

6. Luc Rainville, "It's the Ship!" *Beaufort Gyre Exploration Project*, July 26, 2007, <http://www.whoi.edu/beaufortgyre/dispatch2007/dispatch01.html> (November 3, 2007).

7. Ibid.

Glossary

Beaufort Gyre—A swirling pattern of Arctic water that traps sea ice. Ice floes drifting in the gyre may stay frozen for several years, clumping together to form pack ice.

Beaufort Sea—One of several seas that are a part of the Arctic Ocean. It borders northern Canada and Alaska. It is named after Sir Francis Beaufort, an Irish ocean scientist of the nineteenth century.

boundary layer—A layer of air next to an object's surface. In weather science, it is the layer of the atmosphere closest to the earth's surface.

climate—The average weather for a given place over a long period of time.

Doppler radar—A type of radar used to study weather. By bouncing radio signals off raindrops, bugs, or dust carried in wind, a Doppler radar unit can measure the wind's speed and direction.

electrostatic charge—A buildup of electrons in an object so that it contains more electrons than a nearby object.

equinox—The moment when the sun is lined up directly with the earth's equator. Earth has an equinox twice each year: one in the spring, around March 20, and one in the autumn, around September 23. On an equinox day, every place on Earth gets nearly the same amount of daylight and darkness.

eyewall—A tight wall of cloud ringing the clear center, or eye, of a hurricane.

eyewall replacement cycle—The process by which rain bands in a hurricane sometimes tighten around an eyewall to form a new eyewall, which chokes off and replaces the inner eyewall.

Faraday cage—A metal cage or box that protects people inside it from electricity. It works because the electric current flows across its outer surface. It is named after British physicist Michael Faraday, a pioneer in the understanding of electricity.

floe—A piece of sea ice.

free troposphere—A section of the lower atmosphere that lies above the boundary layer.

global circuit—An electric circuit that surrounds the earth, created by a positive electric charge in the upper atmosphere and a negative charge in the earth's surface.

global warming—A rising trend in the average temperature of the earth's surface. Scientists around the world say global warming is being caused by human activities, mainly by raising the level of carbon dioxide in the atmosphere.

greenhouse gas—A gas that traps heat as a greenhouse does. Carbon dioxide, water vapor, and methane are natural greenhouse gases. Human activities have increased carbon dioxide in the atmosphere by burning fuels that contain carbon, mainly coal and oil.

hurricane—A tropical storm with winds of 74 miles per hour or greater, usually accompanied by rain, thunder, and lightning.

lead (pronounced LEED)—A stretch of open seawater formed when a piece of sea ice cracks open.

McMurdo Station—The largest outpost in Antarctica. It belongs to the United States.

meteorologist—A scientist who studies weather. A meteorologist usually has at least a bachelor's degree in meteorology, the study of weather.

pack ice—Drifting sea ice that has packed together in large masses.

rain bands—Bands of heavy rain and wind that spiral outward from the center of a hurricane.

sea ice—Ice that is formed when ocean water freezes.

tornado—A violent, rotating column of air that reaches from a thunderstorm to the ground.

turbulence—An irregular motion of air that causes a plane to shake when in flight.

typhoon—A hurricane that forms in the western Pacific Ocean.

Further Reading

Books

Hollingshead, Mike, and Eric Nguyen. *Adventures in Tornado Alley: The Storm Chasers*. New York: Thames & Hudson, 2008.

Mehling, Randi. *Weather, and How it Works*. New York: Chelsea House, 2006.

Revkin, Andrew C. *The North Pole Was Here: Puzzles and Perils at the Top of the World*. Boston: Houghton Mifflin, 2006.

Treaster, Joseph B. *Hurricane Force: In the Path of America's Deadliest Storms*. Boston: Kingfisher, 2007.

Vogt, Gregory L. *The Atmosphere: Planetary Heat Engine*. Minneapolis: Twenty-First Century Books, 2007.

Video Resources

Stormchasers. Dir. Greg MacGillivray. Image Entertainment, 2000.

National Geographic: Tornado Intercept. National Geographic Video, 2006.

Internet Addresses

NOAA. "Science with NOAA Research." July 2004.
<http://www.oar.noaa.gov/k12/index.html>

Pew Center on Global Climate Change. "Global Warming—Kids Page."
<http://www.pewclimate.org/global-warming-basics/kidspage.cfm>

UCAR. "Web Weather for Kids."
<http://eo.ucar.edu/webweather/>

Index